MY DINNER WITH

NILS

ALSO BY NILS PETERSON

MY DINNER WITH

NILS

POEMS BY NILS PETERSON

KINCHAFOONEE
CREEK PRESS ⋈ ATHENS, GA

Book design by Norman Minnick
Author photo by Christine Daniel

ISBN: 979-8-218-86850-5

Kinchafoonee Creek Press
585 White Circle #29
Athens, Georgia 30605

www.kcpress.org

BANQUET MENU

Antipasto

Primo

Intermezzo

Secondo

Contorno

Dolce

Antipasto

the year is a road
that turns on its way
where we are seems clear
and maybe next day
but then in its going
it bends out of sight
we follow its flowing
with all our unknowing

all things lament,
for the sun no matter
how brightly it's shone
sends out shadows
at the end of the day
—and Time knows
it too "must have a stop."

THREE SHORT ESSAYS ON LOVE

First Love

Latin class.
Alphabetical seating.
Peterson, Nils.
Desk behind—
Plummer, Patience.
Amo, Amas, Amat.
Pageboy bob. Brown eyes.
Complexion—adolescent.
No words between us.
Her eyes burned holes
into my back.
Too great a gulf.
I'd skipped a grade,
she an older woman.

I did not know who I was
until she taught me desire
and then I did not know who I was.

earth loves the new
enough to kill the old, loves
spring enough to invite
winter, is kind enough
to give us autumn apples
to help some make it
through the long night

last night

I dreamed of an old love
desire each for each deep desperate
we clung with a fierceness
that should have happened years ago

we never got together
but there was a moment in a kitchen
when it was our turn to cook
for others whose turn was to ski

air crackled as we chopped salad
boiled pasta water
looked at each other
til the moment came

but at the same moment
a knock at the door
an uninvited guest
skis over his shoulder
the person from Porlock
who cost Coleridge Xanadu

well, that was that

she's long gone
so very very young
but him I see now and again

I had a good life
with the woman I was married to then
maybe because of his knock
so thanks are in order

but the dream explains why
I've never forgiven him

A SHORT POEM ON THE HUMAN CONDITION

"I'm odd and full of love..."

—Theodore Roethke

My guess is that only the most "unexamined life"
would think upon itself and not find its subject odd.
Certainly we are all singular, and, as the song goes,
"There will never ever be another me."

The next part's harder. "Full of love?" Well, maybe,

"Once in awhile" as another song goes.

As my train chugs off from Then to Whenever,
I can still see you through the dusty window.

You've gotten off at your station
pulled your collar up about your neck.

You're wearing a jaunty hat, give a jaunty wave,
offer a brave smile, and set off on your way,

But this is my train. The conductor has punched
my ticket. My bags are stowed above.

First light and first pee arrive together. Lingering last dream. Find paper. Find pen. Drat. Find one that writes. Hesiod said first there was Chaos. Well, at least something. We say, first there was not even nothing. Then the Big Bang.

PICASSO AND MILES IMPROVISING

They trust the first line is right,
or that the second will make it so...

or the third

SOME CRITICISM, SOME THEORY, SOME QUESTIONS

He said,
"Too much plot, too little dancing."

Plot would have us believe the world
is understandable. Not "The King
died, then the Queen," but
"The King died and the Queen
died of grief."
           We want cause
to break onto the future like
a great wave.
           So, how is it you
woke up where you woke up this morning?
What was the cause and the cause
of that cause? Is your storyline believable?
And why isn't there more dancing?

TOES FOR NORM

How faithful the things of my room,
the bureau, the chest, my heaped
clothing comfortable as a sleeping cat.

They all come back, every morning,
from where they go at night, back
just before me to make up the room
so it is ready when I arrive—and

when I step out to get the morning paper,
the world too is back from its wandering,
ready to do its job. So many things want
to please, whose Beingness pleases—

the long toes at the end of my body,
how elegant they are—even
the one with the blackened nail.

January. Sunday morning. Newspaper filled with Herodish things, yet the sun rises above the cold earth. Roots stir. Somewhere there's music.

I wrote this a few years ago.

> How could the angel
> who left the immensity
> of Always to whisper
> in the ear of the girl child
> go back to the old chorus
> with the other angels?
> So he stayed around watching,
> living like us in before and after,
> now and again humming
> a new song to himself.

I've been thinking about this angel, wondering how he's getting along this year watching us fumble on our way. It must be hard. But I don't think he'd change his mind.

Primo

The first course,
which can include dishes like
risotto or gnocchi

A MEMORABLE FANCY

On the last day of the year, I think about the very first day.

One early morning a Minnesota friend turned his iPhone towards his Minnesota window and we saw snow and a grove of slim, bare trees. He'd been singing, so music was in the air and looking at the beautiful scene I remembered the song, "Morning has broken like the first morning" and I found myself wondering if this is what the first morning looked like.

We think of Eden as summer, everything in bloom, everything perfect and perpetual. A naked Adam and Eve parading around comfortably in their skin suits with navel or without depending on the artist, but suppose the first morning was like this one in Minnesota though the trees, unlike the ones outside my friend's window, would not have lost their leaves—they would not yet have gotten them. Our hibernating friends, bears and moles say, would be created asleep in their caves or little hollows beneath the new trees. They'd soon awaken for the first time—and the seeds and tubers would begin to stir to their unfolding, to the finding out their size, their shapes, their colors—what they'll be when they grow up—fruit, flower, vegetable—the creation a child of time, not a creature of eternity.

Adam and Eve came wholly finished later. They entered time without growing into it. Maybe that was their trouble, our trouble, that separation. Also, God told them it's better not knowing, indeed, ordered them not to know. Perhaps He/She was thinking ahead to Thomas Gray's line, "Where ignorance is bliss, 'Tis folly to be wise." but we chose knowing, we chose folly, marvelous folly, and have learned much, but we have not yet chosen wisdom.

17

THIS BUSINESS OF GETTING OLD

is strange. I went to my last opera a few Sundays ago. The long drive, the long sit and the long drive back are hard on my legs despite the fact that for years I've had the best cheap seat in the house. So, things are different and so much requires so much consciousness. Too much.

My past hangs around hiding in corners ready to leap out and surprise me when I think I'm thinking of something else. Say I'm walking down the street and see a squirrel tightrope-walking across some electric cable. My mind leaps to Patsy Carran, an old girlfriend who brought back to me the phrase "bright-eyed and bushy tailed" the description of the squirrel-child from the Thornton Burgess books I read so many years ago. And then I'm in the apartment above the garage I grew up in when my father was a chauffeur because I borrowed those books, small ones, maybe 3" by 4", beautifully illustrated, from the people who moved into it after my father got a different job and we bought our own house. Then I'm a boy standing in the gravel drive looking at the back of the big house where the rich people lived. So it is almost as if every moment is a kind of time machine.

Faulkner says that for the old "all the past is not a diminishing road but, instead, a huge meadow which no winter ever quite touches, divided from them now by the narrow bottle-neck of the most recent decade of years." Some truth there. Somewhere else I've read that viewing one's past is like looking at your life through the wrong end of a telescope.

Here's an entry in my notebook from I can't remember where, though I know it's a recent reading: "'Memory is a thing of the past,' said Steven's mother sliding into Alzheimer's."

Yet Ann Patchett says, "Coming back is the thing that enables you to see how all the dots in your life are connected." I believe that. And Marilynne Robinson says, "We are part of a mystery, a splendid mystery within which we must attempt to orient ourselves if we are to have a sense of our own nature," and I believe that too.

DEBATING WITH YOUR DOG
ON THE MEANING OF LIFE

I was browsing through a book about poetry the morning
after I had proofread a poem of mine. I came across this
in a discussion of Frost's most famous poem "Stopping by
Woods on a Snowy Evening." You'll remember the speaker
stops his sleigh "between the woods and frozen lake" to sit
for a moment in the lovely, dark, snowy quiet and brood a
bit about deep things, though his horse seems ready to get to
the barn. So it shakes its sleigh bells to urge the speaker on.

The author of the book I was reading says, "The horse
seems endowed with good sense—a go-ahead sort, without
the dreaminess, the romantic wistfulness, of the traveler,
without the sense of failure or deprivation." [William
Logan, *Dickinson's Nerves, Frost's Woods,* 278.] I felt
there was something familiar here, but not from Frost's
poem, and, after a while, I realized that my poem and
Frost's poem were in many ways the same in plot and
theme. So, here's my poem:

"Easter Saturday"

Walking the dog
in a cathedral of an afternoon,
not gothic, roman—sky a blue dome
held up by north south east and west.
Even the distant freeway traffic
sounds hushed like the way we talk
in a place that feels sacred.

The dog, however, is as interested
in earthly things as ever. He gives

a worldly woof then me a look that says
"What is, is. No need to get poetical."
He's got a good case, and, yet,
it is a cathedral of an afternoon.

What didn't specifically say in my poem is that I stopped,
stopped to feel the cathedralness, and in that feeling to
wonder about things. Some notion of awe was there, a
feeling of the sacred, the sacredness of... well you supply
your own answer.

THE BEST MEAL EVER

My mother's father died during, but not because of, the war and so she went back to Sweden on the first possible boat—1946—September leaving my father, brother, and me to get along. I had just started high school, 9th grade, I was soon to be 13.

We had always walked home for lunch, which mother made for us, then back to school. It must have been an hour break and the walk was not short. But now we had to make do. There was a lunch program at the grammar school my brother attended. There was a cafeteria at the high school. If you ate quickly, you could go out and pitch pennies against the curb of the graceful, curved driveway with the other guys—the trick was to toss your penny up close but not to touch the curb. If you did, you lost your coin. If you were closest, you got to pick up all the pennies, which would jingle comfortably in your pocket all afternoon. Maybe "Open the Door, Richard" was the big song.

But some days I would meet my father for lunch. The war had given him a place where his ability could be recognized—and he moved from the maintenance department—his first job with Mack Motors the company he'd joined to help with the war effort passing the chauffeur's job, which he liked, over to Victor Nicholson—to night foreman, to day foreman, to plant manager, this from a man who had to leave school at the age I was at that moment very much boy in and go to work.

So I'd walk out of Plainfield High School, up Park Avenue to the White Tower and my father would drive down to meet me and we lunched side by side—sitting on stools before the counter with other working men—my father dressed now in a suit—and we'd order hamburgers made of thin slices of ground meat, topped with grilled onions and slices of sour pickle. I don't think the world, our world, had yet discovered French fries. The bun was soft. I don't think we added ketchup. Maybe my father did. Fifteen cents they cost, maybe a dime, but the fancy lunch my godmother was cooking for the rich up on Hillside Avenue was not more heavenly than this gritty texture of meat, tart sharp salt taste of pickle, and onions, the onions, a heaven of fried onions—their taste, their smell, the crispness of the ones slightly burned—and sitting there on stools side by side with my father in this lunch heaven of working-male energy, our varied futures waiting outside the door to carry us away when the milky coffee was finished.

I thought of this again today while thinking about Thanksgiving, but I wrote this thirty years ago:

"1990/1946"

Soon I will be older than my father
when he died. How often I've thought—I'm forty.
What was he doing when he was forty?
or forty-five? fifty? when he was this age
or that he was doing... and I would fill in
the blank part memory, part imagination.

Sometimes I see me there too and try
to hold his mind in mine while thinking
back into the mind I wore then—like now,
mother away, I come as my father, day-shift
foreman at Mack Motors and worried about me,
and I come as me just worried, starting high school,
and we meet at the White Tower, eat thin hamburgers,
sliced pickles, comforting fried onions.

But I've been for many years now older than my father was when he died. I've had the real sense of having to go it alone.

DREAMS, THE THEORY OF EVERYTHING

Here is the long sought for theory of everything.

Dreaming began 13½ billion years ago with the big
bang. The universe itself, as it began to unfold, began to
dream. Why? Well, that is the unexplained part of the
explanation of everything.

As each galaxy coalesced into being, it carried with it
the original dream and gave its own shading made out
of its unique balance, its proportion of light, dark matter,
hydrogen atoms and original big bang stuff.

As each sun formed, it took the big bang and the galaxy
dreams and gave them its own spin, a big star has a
different dreaming than a small star though they both
come from the same family tree and carry the dream
DNA of all the dream time that's gone before

and when the sun gathered or spun off the stuff of
planets and became a solar system, each planet took
what it was given and made its own dreams, Mercury
whizzing around the sun dreams differently from
lumbering Jupiter. So place has something to do with
each planet's dreams as well as the matter of its making.

So our earth, third planet of our system, carries the
dreams of big bang, our galaxy, and our sun into its own
dream.

On our planet, the sea has different dreams from the
plains, the mountains different from the valleys
and the whale plunging into the depths dreams

differently from the minnow hugging the shore

the shivering aspen dreams differently from the sturdy oak

and the raven from the bee

and you and I talking in this talking bring to it the
particular stuff of our lives, our parent's lives and of our
ancestor's lives, where they lived, the languages they
spoke, indeed the dreamings of that great tree of life
all the way back to the first bit of primordial soup that
pulled itself together and declared itself to be a self.

And we are selves, yet part of the dream of our place,
our world, our solar system, our galaxy, and the
particular big bang that happens to be the one we live in.

This is the DNA of our dreaming and the theory of
everything.

THE SECRET RIVER OF ONE'S LIFE

One of the easy metaphors, easy because it just feels
true, is that life is like a river in its flowing from then
to whenever. We are both a leaf floating on it, and the
river itself. Boat maybe. Raft more likely. But those who
know such things say there is a river beneath the river,
the hyporheic flow. "This is the water that moves under
the stream, in cobble beds and old sandbars. It edges up
the toe slope to the forest, a wide unseen river that flows
beneath the eddies and the splash. A deep invisible river,
known to its roots and rocks, the water and the land
intimate beyond our knowing. It is the hyporheic flow I'm
listening for." The person speaking is Robin Kimmerer, a
biologist, professor and member of the Citizen Potawatomi
Nation. It's from her book *Braiding Sweetgrass*.

I've used the river image often enough in my own writing
when thinking about my life and the lives of others, but
now I'm wondering if what I was really trying to do was
to find a way to listen to this deeper river, to get a sense
of it as it winds its way to, well, Is there such a thing as
the hyporheic sea? There must be and therefore all my sea
images really float on that sea beneath the sea. Robin says,
"One thing I've learned in the woods is that there is no such
thing as random. Everything is steeped in meaning, colored
by relationships, one thing with another." Well, yes. This
is the poet's understanding too, and I think it is the basic
understanding of language, maybe of consciousness.

I'm thinking now of a girl I dated my junior year in college.
I had to come back to school a little early because I sang
in the choir and there was a special program early that we
had been asked to sing for. The football team also came
back early for its fall practice. This girl in addition to being

27

a singer was a cheerleader. It worked out that fall that she went out with me every other weekend. A football player took her out the in-between weeks. I was a year younger than my class and very shy. I had just started to do things on the campus, act in plays, write for the newspaper, join the creative writing, finding out how much I loved literature. I enjoyed talking with her. Maybe we held hands, but the truth was she awed me. I was continually surprised she was out with me.

There was a moment, at the end of a date, when I thought I needed to put my arm around her and hold her. I'm not sure I thought as far ahead as a kiss. Hopefully I did. We, it seems so unlikely but this is what I remember, were in a graveyard near the woman's campus sitting on a memorial piece, a rectangular piece of cemetery cement the right height, but I didn't put my arm around her, we talked some more, then I walked her back to the dorm and soon she was going out every week with the football player. We had been together enough to exchange Christmas gifts. I don't remember what I gave her, but she gave me a tan cashmere scarf and a pair of leather gloves both of which I treasured a long time.

So, I'm trying to understand how I ended up living the life I led. I got married nine years after I graduated. I think I likely was the last one of the men in my class to marry. There were some who never married.

Considerations. Likely I was a year younger than she since I'd skipped year. Another consideration, this was 1953 and sort of the unspoken sense in the air was that you'd graduate from college, get a job, get married, and then set off living a sensible adult life something like your parents but better. I had chosen to major in English and would this year choose to minor in philosophy. These were joyful choices, the right choices. I had not started to worry about how I was going to go earning a living. When I got to be a senior (where there was another girl with whom I was less shy, but that's another story), I realized I could put off choosing because all of us guys had to go into the army. The draft was active, though the Korean war was over or about over, I'll have to check dates. My plan was to volunteer to be drafted to get it over with, do my time, get the GI bill and go to grad school maybe in an undefined writer's way. Well, I turned out to be 4F from a bad knee from basketball. There I was with no money, no plans, no career, and as it turned out later, no (other) girl.

So, back to my cemetery moment. Say I had put my arm around the first girl. Say I kissed her. Say we really got serious. What would the consequences have been? I would have had to think about getting a serious job. Maybe one alternative would have been that she worked while I went to school. Yes, but what would I have gone to school for? Likely a teaching credential and likely a high school teaching job somewhere in Kentucky where all of this drama was taking place. That was a most likely river of life, to go back to my original image.

And it might have been a very happy river. But...

there was this other river, "a deep invisible river," the "hyporheic flow" of my life. It needed me to feel my way around for a few years. It needed me to work in the circulation department of the local newspaper for a while, look around that world and decide it was not for me. It needed me to be friends with my parent's Lutheran minister, though I didn't really think of myself as a member of his congregation. (I did help out. Sing now and again in the choir when they needed an extra bass, direct the Sunday School's Christmas play.) When Upsala College,

I'm in New Jersey now living with my parents, needed an Assistant Director of Admission and Choir Manager, he recommended me for the job. I got it, and found I liked college life, the people there, the good talk in the faculty dining room. I read all of Faulkner, thought of myself as a prose person, sat in on a few classes. Since I was managing the choir, I arranged my schedule so I could sing with them as I had in my college choir. One of my jobs was to go around summers to Lutheran summer camps and try to convince young Swedes to come to this college.

At the end of two years, I decided this was a job really wasn't for me anymore. I handed my resignation in a few months early. When my term was over, I still didn't know how I wanted to earn a living. At the end, with no prospect in sight, I gathered my papers up, drove down to Rutgers in New Brunswick, applied to graduate school. My "hyporheic flow" insisted that when I registered I stood next to Ed Kessler, a poet who had begun publishing in good places. We became roommates and sat long nights at the Corner Tavern talking about poems and I learned so much about how to read them. More than in my classes. In truth, in many classes the reading assignments were better than the class.

There were married men living comfortably in "married student's housing" with working wives bringing in money of which I had little. Sometimes I envied them, but they envied the tavern talk time. One tried to join one night when the talk went on all night and moved from tavern to our room. His homecoming was not happy. (One classmate's wife was in a laundromat when a strange crew came in and asked her which pile of clothes was the whitest. She looked down in a rather snooty way and said "that one" and consequently received a royalty check every month for a couple of years. That would have been nice. I could have looked snooty. I likely would have chosen the wrong pile.)

To start again, almost 30 years ago I went to Minneapolis to help celebrate the poet Robert Bly's 65th birthday. One of the other celebrants was James Hillman, renowned psychologist and author. He had co-edited a couple of poetry anthologies with Robert. We sat together waiting for a car to take us to the airport. He asked me what I did for a living. I replied I taught Shakespeare. He then asked me the astonishing question, "How has your life made you ready to teach Shakespeare?"

I was a Shakespeare teacher by accident. Poetry was my assumed province. But one day the head of the department opened the door of his office as I walked by, saw me and he asked me if I would like to teach Shakespeare next semester because the regular teacher had just received a sabbatical. I said sure and I taught it for the next 30 years even on closed circuit television to satellite campuses. I wasn't prepared for it except for teaching a couple of his plays to freshman English classes as a teaching assistant. I didn't take the graduate class in Shakespeare because I didn't like the teacher, though I did take a year of Non-Shakespearean Elizabethan drama from a teacher I liked. But as I thought about his question, it seemed as if my whole life had set me up for saying "sure" and being ready to do it. I was astonished to think it wasn't an accident, it was destiny, my life finding a shape appropriate to it.

Here is a quotation from Hillman's *The Soul's Code* in which he presents the "acorn theory."

> So, too, the image in the acorn. You are born with
> a character; it is given; a gift, as the old stories say,
> from the guardians upon your birth.

I think the first step is the realization that each of us has such a thing. And then we must look back over our lives and look at some of the accidents and curiosities and oddities and troubles and sicknesses and begin to see more in those things than we saw before. It raises questions, so that when peculiar little accidents happen, you ask whether there is something else at work in your life. It doesn't necessarily have to involve an out-of-body experience during surgery, or the sort of high-level magic that the new age hopes to press on us. It's more a sensitivity, such as a person living in a tribal culture would have: the concept that there are other forces at work. A more reverential way of living.

I suggest that when you are thinking about those "peculiar little accidents [that] happen" you are brooding over the "hyporheic flow" of your life, and that it is "a more reverential way of living."

All of this got written because a few mornings ago I woke to a remembrance of that girl in the cemetery. She had had things, serious things, to say to me almost 50 years ago and wanted me to remember. Here she is.

"Once I Went With a Girl Too Beautiful"

Once I went with a girl too beautiful
for me. It was a relief not to have to haggle
with the nickels and dimes of my poor heart.
She was too much. I did not even make
a pass I was that dumb partly out of my own
nature, but partly having been struck so.
I watched, rather, in awe at the way flesh
transfigures itself by hanging right.
Now and then I would wonder what

is she doing out with me? I had no answer;
so, when she got engaged to the co-captain
of the football team, my hurt was real,
but the ending seemed right, my sense of plot
   satisfied.
            The scene changes. 20 years later. London.
Wife and daughters in California—perhaps lost
to me. I have started reading Jung. Sort of
interested. One night in a dream my beautiful
woman comes back, I again in college trying
to do better. I meet her in the street. We talk
politely, then I start to go. She calls out,
      Look at me,
      but I keep going.
      She cries out,
      LOOK AT ME
      I stop, turn,
and see my old girl reclothed and queenly
the dress of her desiring swirling about
like a summer night when every star,
wanting to be no less than itself, lets
its light full on, and I tried, at last,
my absolute best to look at her.

And here, A quotation from the first chapter of Hillman's
book:

There is more in a human life than our theories of
it allow. Sooner or later something seems to
call us onto a particular path. You may remember
this "something" as a signal moment in childhood
when an urge out of nowhere, a fascination, a
peculiar turn of events struck like an annunciation:
This is what I must do, this is what I've got to have.
This is who I am.

CROW'S NEST

Been haunted by the image of a crow's nest lately, the one on top of the tallest mast of an old sailing ship, and thinking about the first time one climbed up to it, maybe you're 12 or 13, the bosun's sent you aloft, rope ladder after rope ladder, up and up, and soon you're 150 ft up on a swaying perch looking down at a swaying sea.

Isn't this like aging? One climbs up a swaying rope ladder of year after year and all of a sudden you're 86 swaying above a sea of years.

I come to the image by way of *Treasure Island,* actually a poem by Seamus Heaney I like a lot that refers to *Treasure Island.* Here is the stanza I'm thinking of now, the final stanza of "In the Attic":

> As I age and blank on names,
> As my uncertainty on stairs
> Is more and more the lightheadedness
>
> Of a cabin boy's first time on the rigging,
> As the memorable bottoms out
> Into the irretrievable...

Yes, yes, "uncertainty on stairs" and "As the memorable bottoms out / Into the irretrievable..."

In the poem, he's standing in the attic of his old childhood house and looks out of the window at a birch tree, planted as a sapling, when Memory brings the ghost of his grandfather who brings a ghost of "Treasure Island," and the speaker finds himself for a moment both young and old:

A birch tree planted twenty years ago
Comes between the Irish Sea and me
At the attic skylight, a man marooned
In his own loft, a boy
Shipshaped in the crow's nest of a life...

At a certain age, everything has a touch of elegy. It is not
depressing, just a sense of where the world is and where
you are in it. And memory, that old friend, moves from the
neighborhood into a senior residence and visits you when
it can, leaving me this morning feeling like

...a boy
Shipshaped in the crow's nest of a life.

HOW WE LEARN TO WRITE POEMS

Three attempts at the mystery.

FROM THE NOVEL *THOMAS MURPHY* BY ROGER ROSENBLATT

The farmer-fisher-father of the title character, a successful poet on a level of Heaney and Muldoon, is reading to the boy Thomas Murphy.

"His favorite was Yeats. He'd read me the early poems, easier for a boy to understand, such as "At Galway Races," "These Are the Clouds," and "Brown Penny." He loved "Brown Penny"—a young man's poem, he said—and he recited it from memory. Lusty, wistful, plain sad sometimes, as he'd glance at his left leg, then at the space where his right leg used to be. He lost that one in a thresher, when he was 18. He never complained, never a word, just that glance at the absent leg. More than the books, that taught me how to write a poem."

ROBERT BLY

One of the joys of reading Robert Bly is that one is always learning something about writing. Awareness grows larger, your field of understanding suddenly has more acres. As a writer, my favorite poem in his book *Talking into the Ear of a Donkey* is "My Father at Forty," particularly the last three lines. (I don't think it's the best poem in the book, just the one I learned the most from about the whys and ways of writing.)

36

The way I found
Of opening a poem I took
From the way he walked into a field.

WHAT MY FATHER TAUGHT ME, MAYBE

He had a sharp eye, though one was better than the other.
He could look down a long board, squint his less good
eye, and the good one would show him the slightest bit of
warping. Maybe this is what I learned from him. I look
down a line of poetry and my good eye can see where it's
warped. Then I try to see if it can be made to do the job or
if I must discard it for better.

FACING THE MUSIC

I

End of a strange day. Sitting with a drink, listening to
jazz vocals, old songs, talking slow, the way one does at
such an hour. Particularly if one's companion is one's self.
Melancholic but mellow. Sipping a vintage of old age at
l'heure bleue.

And from Tony Bennett

Someday, when I'm awfully low
When the world is cold
I will feel a glow just thinking of you
And the way you look tonight

But it's an old Bennett making a quick grab at the high
notes and almost getting there—though still comfortable
and easy with the sway of word and music. The Someday
here for us both. One knows about the dementia. No Lady
Gaga in this version to help. Just old age dealing as well
as it can with pitch and memory and vision—and singing,
and yes, singing, and yes, one thinks of Yeats:

An aged man is but a paltry thing,
A tattered coat upon a stick, unless
Soul clap its hands and sing, and louder sing
For every tatter in its mortal dress…

For his 75th birthday, Dave Brubeck invited a bunch of
"Young Tigers and Old Lions" to a recording studio and
composed and recorded an original celebration of each.
The only unoriginal melody was the second track, "How
High the Moon," sung by Jon Hendricks—bringing his

now old man's voice—all the bassness out of it, but not soprano—thin, quavery, black. He sings "Somewhere there's heaven, it's where you are"—and yes, we believe it—that there is one and it's where she, whoever she might be, is—Dave Brubeck rumbles beneath in sweet elegiac support. The more Hendricks' voice lost, the more beautiful it became—is there a blessing then in loss, a wisdom? A young critic says it's too slow, takes too long, but young critics are too impatient to hear well.

And now Sinatra's "Send in the Clowns," the truth of a special longing in his voice not the strutting bluff stuff of "I Did it My Way" way. More the regret of "losing my timing so late in my career." Maybe it's about Ava. I'd like to think so.

Back to the "Someday" which is today,

> Lovely, never, never change
> Keep that breathless charm
> Won't you please arrange it?
> 'Cause I love you
> Just the way you look tonight

And whoever she might be is here again with her all her "breathless charm."

She was first here for me when I was a boy listening to the radio and the verse above was the theme song for an advertisement for a face cream. So I heard it again and again. I'm glad I can't remember the name of the face cream.

p.s. I'm eleven or twelve, had heard Sinatra or Como croon "September Song," but over the crackly Philco comes Walter Huston half-singing, half-talking "but it's

39

a long, long time from May to December / And the days grow short...." Something of me understood it was a voice, an old man's voice, sounding of truth and dry leaf, not a baritone making pretty music.

II

Fred & Ginger Face the Music

A single rose in a white vase on the table—a long, languid gracefulness. It's Fred Astaire, I think for moment and remember the last 10 minutes of an old movie.

Fred had joined the Navy to escape Ginger. Why that would be so, I can't imagine. However, at movie's end, Ginger's in a gorgeous flowing gown, Fred, white tie and tails. She's leaning on some kind of column, looking away, far away, far far away—working hard at moving on.

There's music. Fred glides over, does a turn. She ignores him. Another turn, she ignores him. At Fred's third turn, Ginger's body moves. She hasn't moved it. It has moved of itself and carried Ginger along with it. Soon they're dancing. Soon the music makes Fred sing,—"There may be trouble ahead / But while there's moonlight / And music and love and romance / Let's face the music and dance."

That's such a good place to stop, but I can't. The bridge carries me over, well, you can fill in with the rainbow if you wish, "Soon we'll be without the moon / Humming a different tune and then"... and then the verse, "There may be teardrops to shed / So while there's moonlight / And music and love and romance / Let's face the music and dance." What a wonderful way to use that old contrary phrase, "Let's face the music."

If we're going to have to face the music, let's face it with a dance.

Good advice.

Footnote. No one seems to know the origin of the phrase "Face the Music." One theory has it that it was advice to an actor who had stage fright, the sense being that you faced the orchestra pit and said or sang your lines. Seems like a long stretch to me. Another comes from British military life. When you disgraced your regiment, you were drummed out of it, drummers ominously beating some solemn steady beat while you marched in front of your former comrades so they could see your disgrace. The trouble with this is that the phrase seems to have originated in America.

Nevertheless, caught up in my Fred Astaire fantasies, I imagined him being drummed from the corps for something like making a not-unwelcomed pass at the Colonel's daughter and being kicked out. I hear the solemn drumbeat and then halfway to his exit he smiles, stops marching, gives his feet over to a jazzy syncopation against the drumbeat and taps his way out the door. He turns, gives an impudent salute, exits, who knows, maybe to run off with the colonel's daughter and the two of them face the music and dance. Of course the daughter would be played by Ginger in the movie version of this footnote.

III

Thinking of Fred and Ginger, I was sad because I had not danced with Judith more.

She was a great dancer and enjoyed it so. I was a clumsy

partner, having grown up in an age where there were defined dances with particular steps you were supposed to take and I never learned them. They offered lessons in the 7th grade, but you had to ask a partner. I did ask the girl behind me and she hit me over the head with her spelling book as I recall. In high school there was a dance that I spent in the cloakroom unwilling to come out though lovely women kept coming in and asking me to. The first time I ever danced was as a freshman in college. I had asked this girl out on a date, Alice Moss was her name. I think we went to a movie, but when we got back her dorm was holding a dance. There was no way of admitting I'd never danced before so out we went on the dance floor and I clutched her and moved my feet. Well, nothing much happened. We moved around the floor a bit and then went and sat down. The dorm threw us all out at 10, so I went back to my dorm relieved that that was over.

But then dancing became something that if you could move your feet in time to the music, you could manage. So I found I could manage.

When I was courting Judith, I visited her at her parent's home in Maryland and she took me to a party with her old high school friends and they were all doing a new thing called "The Twist." I was now a stuffy graduate student who hadn't danced in years and I was a little appalled. But the terrible thing was that I enjoyed the pose of being appalled. Well, we commit many strange sins along life's way. In the middle of the night or at the end of the right movie, we remember.

But there was one time when I was applauded for dancing with Judith. After I had retired we went on a few cruises with friends and after dinner there were dances and so we danced and I enjoyed it. I didn't have to do much. Judith did it all. In fact, with my advancing neuropathy there was a time she had to prop me up a little. I started using a cane and, at our last cruise, it was clear that I could not venture out on the dance floor without possibly falling down. But Judith wanted to dance, and, yes, by this time I wanted to dance with her. So, I leaned against a column that held up the roof and reached out my hand. She took it and did a graceful turn. I swayed in time to the music supported by the column and Judith danced out and back, out and back in a lovely way. At the end, the other dancers applauded.

Intermezzo

LUCILLE CLIFTON READS MY PALM

We sit together on a rock and Lucille
takes my long thin white hand
in her warm thick black one
and holds it shutting her eyes for a moment. Then,

"Your hand is delicate for a big man's
like my son who lifts weights but is gentle,
so gentle. Sometimes I can see which parent
moved one the most in a life. Yours was
your mother—I don't know if for good
or for bad. You have lived your life
in fits and starts, beginning again and again.
I don't often get aunts, but you
have an aunt who cares for you and wants you to know
she thinks you're doing OK.
There is a sadness about you. I would like
to say it will get better. I would like to,
but I can't. You may be one of those
who just must learn to live somehow
in sorrow, though sometimes joy
is a friend of such sorrow."

coast road

north and north   red glare
of sinking sun spread wide
across the westward sea

inland trees, hills, tiny houses,
magicking into silhouettes,
even my voice, a silhouette

I try to remember an old tune,
"Just a song at twilight
when the lights are low"

no one in the car but me
and you who are not here
save as a "flickering shadow"

which "softly comes and goes"
on my right a full moon rises
behind streaks of blown clouds

my little car knows its way
on this fulcrum of a road between
light rising and sinking,

and I, though not content, am
content to let it carry me along
to where it would have me go

waking orange-pink room mirror swinging
on oak bison horns above an oak dresser
3:00 AM hotel I pee guiltily in the corner
wash basin then pull the curtains aside—

bleak black empty asphalt crooked
sidewalks lone street light rain
slanting before the flat red rectangles
of opposing buildings and suddenly I'm

a drummer with a line of collar buttons,
hairpins, celluloid dickies, caught in
the gray walls of a seacoast town, needing
to place some merchandise to make it home.

I lie back on my narrow bed and think how
this country was built of bricks of loneliness.

The seagull flies white and sharply defined
above the mirroring inlet, but I look down
at its shadow deep in the low tidal water
where its shape is complicated and muddy.
I love both, what is discrete and clear and
what is muddy and shape-changing.

Secondo

"HE WORDS ME GIRLS, HE WORDS ME"

Reading into and about Wallace Stevens this morning
I find this quotation, "The deepening need for words
to express our thoughts and feelings... loving them and
feeling them, makes us search for the sound of them, for
a finality, a perfection, an unalterable vibration...." I'm
an endless rewriter and surely this is part of the reason
for that, getting the sound exactly right even if it means a
shift in meaning, but I thought as I read those words of my
first pure experience of the delight in sound divorced from
meaning. I should add as an adult because I loved word-
sounds as a child "Hey diddle diddle," "with a knick-
knack paddy whack," Rumpelstiltskin.

At this time I was sitting at my desk working as Assistant
Director of Admissions at Upsala College in East Orange,
New Jersey [auto-correct wanted to make it Upscale
College which it wasn't] reading a lot of Faulkner in my
spare time, thinking of myself essentially a fiction person
though I had written some traditional poems and had
bouts of strange love with one poem and another. A phrase
out of nowhere flew in one ear and almost out the other
before I managed to catch it, "crew went the curlew as it
flew in a curlicue." I can't explain the delight it gave me. I
loved the sound of it, the shape of it, the feel of it though
clearly it was meaningless. But meaning was irrelevant. I
don't know if I wrote it down, but memory found some
way of retaining it. I would take it out now and then and
feel it, almost like pebble one finds at a beach and carries
in a pocket for a while for comfort.

Almost sixty years later, I found a place to put it. I was
poet laureate of Santa Clara County in California. There
were half a dozen other laureates around and we were

going to do a reading together. I suggested that it would be fun to all write something of the same kind and suggested a piece of exactly 100 words. It could be prose or lined, whatever shape or form, but it had to be exactly 100 words including the title. The ocean of words and word combination possibilities is so large that some kind of shape-giving limitation is a gift not a handicap. By making things harder, it makes things easier. Here's what I wrote:

"A Small Bang"

Syllables pour into a hundred-word universe shocked as the first hydrogen atoms. Each has a music. They circle, join, suddenly—word sounds— "Crew went the curlew as it flew in a curlicue." They rhyme. "Ache did" pairs with "naked." They gather into galaxies, "He did not know who he was until she taught him desire, then he did not know who he was," until here at the end of the Dictionary of the Milky Way, we dangle from a participle, aware of dark matter, what has not as yet been seen, so not as yet said.

[I wonder now if it should end "what has not as yet been said, so not as yet seen." Just a morning wonderment.]

The more I read this, the prouder I am of it and glad that my old bit of sound joy at last had a home. How my koan about desire got in there I'm not sure, but I'm proud of it too though my pride derives from sense as well as sound.

I'll add as a little footnote here, in my collection *All the Marvelous Stuff* there is a gathering called the Book of Scheherazade. This is the opening poem. The gathering consists of ten hundred-word pieces and one more word, the word I think of as the most important in the language, in any language. You'll have to go there to find out what it is. You'll remember that Scheherazade saved her life by telling stories for a thousand and one nights.

P.S.

I want to end this by giving you the full Stevens quotation that began this piece. "The deepening need for words to express our thoughts and feelings which, we are sure, are all the truth that we shall ever experience, having no illusions, makes us listen to words when we hear them, loving them and feeling them, makes us search for the sound of them, for a finality, a perfection, an unalterable vibration, which it is only within the power of acutest poet to give them…" from "The Noble Rider and the Sound of Words."

The middle of the sentence gives much to think about.

ON VACATION, THINKING OF YEATS

Yeats has been a life-long companion for me, his long, mostly unfulfilled love for Maude, his strange interests in the occult, his lovely lyricism sometimes approaching but never quite falling into sentimentality, the music of his rhythms. In more practical ways too. Once I was teaching "Among School Children" shortly after a birthday and realized that I was now a "sixty-year-old smiling man," his momentary awareness and mine were one. Last week I was on vacation with my daughters and their partners (and for a short while my grandson). We had rented for a week a stunning house with a great several-acred backyard sloping down to Puget Sound. There was a small apple orchard with wonderful apples and outside my bedroom window (A room with an enormous walk-in closet, an attached 20-foot-long bathroom with an enormous footed tub, and an attached sunroom fitted out as a writing room with desk and daybed) was an enormous maple, tall, tall with a trunk at least 4 feet thick at the bottom. We had some marvelous severe weather and it was a treat to lie in bed at night and see and hear the great limbs and leaves thrash about.

We were there from the end of September into the beginning of October. Many of the trees had put on their autumn clothing and the Yeats line "The trees are in their autumn beauty" came to my mind from "The Wild Swans at Coole." I have a program that is filled with wonderful things and so I downloaded all of Yeats (with pictures) and turned to that poem. You may remember the opening stanza,

> The trees are in their autumn beauty,
> The woodland paths are dry,

Under the October twilight the water
Mirrors a still sky;
Upon the brimming water among the stones
Are nine-and-fifty swans

He's feeling older and out of it (He started feeling older
when he was very young) than when he first saw them,
but they still seem the same. This was before he finally got
married (not Maude) and started an almost second life.

Unwearied still, lover by lover,
They paddle in the cold
Companionable streams or climb the air;
Their hearts have not grown old;
Passion or conquest, wander where they will,
Attend upon them still.

But there are 9 and 50 swans, so clearly one swan no
longer has a partner though he flies with the rest of them.
So, I found myself thinking of me about to start my 88th
year (much older than Yeats got to) as the 59th swan.
Judith has been gone a year and a half and one of the
reasons we chose this location was so we could go over
easily to the place where Judith is buried on Bainbridge
Island, one of the few places where a green burial is
allowed. We went twice. It is a beautiful place, a small
meadow surrounded by forest, a sweet pond with ducks
just below her site. I can't actually get out to see her place
with its level-to-the-ground stone with my name on it too
because the slope is too severe for me and my walker. So
I watched my daughters and their 2 dogs frolic around
through an open car window and looked at the photos
they took and sent. It is very peaceful there and I felt part
of the great peace.

It took a lot of engineering and a lot of equipment to get

me to where we are staying and have me be comfortable. I was worried about it. But Erika is a great manager and so she got me into the car along with my walker and my chair that raises up and down and has brakes and skitters about as I propel it with my legs and my footstool so I could get dressed in the morning, and my back rest so I could sleep with an upward slant and charger cables for all of the paraphernalia that makes up a modern life.

I once wrote "Nils is in his autumn beauty," but added, truthfully, it's winter.

POETRY OF THE '60S

The older you get, the harder it is to understand how long ago was yesterday. At the end of the '50s and early '60s poets, beats and not so beat, were delighted to discover that a poem did not have to be high-toned and Greco-Roman referenced to be a poem. The field of possibility became wider, a straitjacket of high seriousness had been taken off, an element of low play was welcomed, not looked down upon. I was looking yesterday into a 60-year-old collection called *A First Reader of Contemporary American Poetry*. It's filled with things I delighted in then and still do, but it is hard to deal with the fact that what I still think of as contemporary poetry is now more than half a century old. One of the delights of then was Eugene Lesser. Here's a poem of his.

"A Poem for Everybody"

You get that end of the road feeling, you know?
Over the hill, past your prime,
on the way out, washed up, a has-been,
dethroned, usurped, subsumed,
a shadow of your former self.
You see the handwriting on the wall.
You throw in the towel.
You can't cut the mustard.
You gird your loins for permanent obscurity,
take pipe, eat crow.

But as subtle and final and
irrevocable and certain and
unmistakable as it is,
the knowledge comes on you
suddenly, in an instant.

One day, clipping your toenails,
you stare into the abyss.
Like the way Victor Mature felt
the first time a producer told him
that to appear in a film as a cool stud
making it with, say, Ann-Margret
would lack verisimilitude.

Well, this is a poem that if it were in a now-contemporary anthology, it would have to be footnoted. Who are these people, Victor Mature and Ann-Margret?

Here's a challenge for you out there. First, do you remember Victor Mature and Ann-Margret? If this were your poem and you were working on it today, what names would you substitute for this pair? Or, maybe you could use an older woman and younger man, or... at this time of history, the possibilities are many.

I will add that the first time I realized I was getting older was when I saw a rerun of *High Society* and thought, well, Bing Crosby really isn't too old for Grace Kelly.

LETTER TO A FRIEND ON MEETING JUDITH

Well I'm reading about the East Coast weather and hoping that it has not gone as far south as Kentucky. I remember reading about you being snowed in for so long. Hope this isn't a repeat, though you said it was cold a week ago. Sorry I haven't gotten back to you sooner. I've just been caught up in a myriad of things, writing, readings, singing, some family business, it all has quieted now. Judith off for a hike, I'm back from my hour long and demanding Pilates class (which I do 3 times a week to keep me somewhat limber. Actually I'm pretty good from knee to elbow. It is the extremities that my kind of neuropathy attacks and my extremities are very far away. Wiggling my toes (autocorrect just changed my toes into thesis. I can't believe it. Clearly I must proofread.) is like sending messages to that space capsule that just landed on a comet. Anyway, I paste as a quotation the dedication to my book *A Walk to the Center of Things* as a way of explaining how Judith and I got together.

"Dedication"

Fifty years ago I was standing mallet in hand by a croquet court at the Breadloaf Writers Conference needing a partner. A young woman, also a waiter, walked by. She was wearing Bermuda shorts. Two years later, we were married.

This book is dedicated to the great, overarching fact of that marriage, wide enough and long enough to give room to the many small marriages and separations that allowed us to grow.

So that is how it began. We were both waiters at the

Breadloaf Writer's Conference in 1961. You may know it was started by Robert Frost and held at a camp owned by Middlebury College in Middlebury, Vermont. He was alive then and there, though he died later that fall. He seemed very, very old, though, in truth, he was not much older than I am now. There were other well-known writers there too. The poets John Ciardi (who now ran the conference and was the reason I was there since he was the writer in residence at Rutgers), Howard Nemerov, a favorite poet of mine and my doubles partner for the conference, JF Nims, whose "Love Poem" is one of my all-time favorites, and others. One of my favorite writers who became for a while something of a friend was the author of *Revolutionary Road*. Hopefully his name will appear by the end of this note though it's not here now. [I'm proofreading and it's still not here though I can see his face. It will come sometime and I'll send it on.] [Richard Yates] Being a waiter was really a work scholarship, but it made you a member of the staff instead one of the paying guests which was a big shift for the better in status.

Anyway, there I was standing by the croquet court with Tanya and Wyman looking for a partner when Judith came by. I asked her and it all began. It could not have been at a more romantic place. Beautiful New England scenery, woods and waterfalls, an enormous amount of drinking and carrying on. The days began with Bloody Marys to help one sober up from the night before. The talk was good. the readings fine and the gemutlichkeit, well, I can't even imagine better. One thing that happened is that one of the waiters had set one of Robert Frost most famous poems to music and he heard about it and we were asked to perform it at the big banquet the last night when literary mucky mucks arrived from NYC and Boston to celebrate. (Archibald Macleish was one.) Anyway, Frost's face grew longer and longer as we sang "stopping by woods on a

snowy evening" to the tune of "Hernando's Hideaway."
I was 27, Judith as she told me, was "almost twenty."
Nothing serious could happen to me there, clearly.

We're in another COVID lockdown at my senior center and
so I'm trying to get people at my senior residence started
writing memoirs as a way of making use of this time.
Today I'm suggesting as a prompt bits of conversations
that have stayed with them—like the phrase above and like
when I took Judith out for a drink on what was our first
date. (It's possible I didn't even think of it that way.) When
we sat at the bar waiting to order our drinks she said, "I'm
almost twenty." The memory brings with it my surprise as
well as the look of the Vermont bar, a long narrow room
with tables by the window and, yes, even the dress that
she wore, a light blue frock she referred to as her Swedish
dress. I'm guessing her mother made her take one good
outfit just in case. At the time we were there, Robert Frost
was there too.

Tanya and Wyman had a lovely apartment in NYC and
several of us, Judith included, went and spent a couple of
days there sleeping in heaps on their living room floor and
we tooled around NY. I took Judith to my favorite elegant
smorgasbord place, The Stockholm. When she looked
at the long table loaded with food, the first 5 feet or so
loaded with varieties of anchovies and sardines many of
which still had their eyes in their heads, Judith looked up
at me and said, "Nils, I'm not as sophisticated as you think
I am." Well, the upshot of it was that she had fallen in love
with me, and though I liked her and thought her cute, I,
obtuse with women as always, thought that nothing special
had happened. I won't go into all the details of the next 2
years as we wrote back and forth and visited each other
off and on during holidays. She was attending a small
woman's college in Milwaukee, My graduate school was

in New Brunswick, NJ. So, we didn't see each other that often. I visited her home outside of Washington DC. She was scheduled to visit my parent's home in Ohio (that's where they were living then. I too for a short while.), but my father died a month or so before, but she came anyway and somehow that felt good.

Finally I decided that we needed to end it, but that didn't turn out to be so easy to do, though we did break up and she found a friend who was a painter, and I found a girl in the library whom I liked. At last, however, I thought it was time for us to be really together, proposed, got accepted. I was totally broke. We honeymooned in NYC on the couple hundred dollars we got as gifts for our wedding which was held at her house, her mother doing all the work. I had a 6-week stint at summer school at Rutgers and a job in California. We piled all our stuff into the biggest, cheapest car I could find. I didn't have the money for a car at the end of my graduate career, so we had to buy one taking out a loan from the credit union. When we headed west, stopping in Ohio where my mother still lived to pile in more stuff, we had to use my father-in-law's gasoline credit card to get there.

We got pregnant on the way. Judith, whose father was an outdoorsman and executive in the Forest Service, insisted that we try camping on the way. I disliked camping which shocked her since in her family male and camping were synonymous. We arrived in San Jose with enough money for one night in a hotel and one day to find a place to stay because we had just enough money to put down a month's deposit. We ended up, through great good fortune and Judith's insistence that the ordinary affordable apartments won't do, in a little cottage on a rich man's estate out in the country and up in the mountains. We could use the swimming pool in the yard, but not the one in his house.

We stayed there for 5 years, though it got lonelier and lonelier for a woman with 2 small children whose husband went off to teach 5 days a week. When I got tenure, we bought a house in the valley which was surrounded by plum orchards but we're now surrounded by apartments and other houses.

So, there you are. A thumbnail sketch. I see that I've neglected all the wonderful times we had together during those 2 difficult years particularly when she would visit me at Rutgers and played around with my graduate school friends or again wandering around NY. Well, you know how exciting it could be from your year there. And in our first 5 years here, Judith got an MA in English and did some teaching and some acting. She taught at a community college for awhile, was a potter for awhile and we'd haul stuff to street fairs and shows. but ended up being a psychotherapist in the Jungian tradition, a tradition whose sense of the nature of the psyche has been of incredible help to us both. She still keeps a small practice going in her office tucked away behind our garage.

Well, not exactly my life story, but a bunch of stuff here.

Again, I hope you're not freezing your gizzard off. I had a nice letter from Lynn Turner yesterday filled with her memories of our days together (quite fun, we shared many of the same traits) and I had a nice note from Marty Diem the week before. Well, now I must proofread and go practice some music for tonight's rehearsal. Fondly, Nils.

In addition to it being Bloomsday, it is the day when Judith and I are celebrating our 53rd anniversary.

My best man, Jack Dubrovsky, was Jewish. He and his wife were good friends of mine through graduate school.

She was my classmate at Rutgers in New Jersey. He was a businessman, broad-shouldered, muscular and rather quick-tempered.

Judith and I were married at her parent's house in Wheaton, Maryland, a suburb of DC. They came down from New Jersey, and decided to sightsee a bit before the ceremony which was to take place in the early afternoon. Well, the time came, and there was no best man. I sat in the basement by myself. All of the guests were upstairs. Judith's mother and my mother getting more and more frantic. The maid kept bringing me bourbon to help pass the time away. At last they arrived, both breathless, Jack a little disheveled.

What happened was that during their tour, they ran into a demonstration led by George Lincoln Rockwell. It was, of course, the American Nazi Party. Words were spoken between Jack and one of the demonstrators, then shoves, at last fists and police and my best man was dragged away. No cell phones or anything of the sort at that time.

He was not held that long. The police were very understanding. Nevertheless....

Well, that was only the first hitch in 53 years of hitches and blessings. I guess that is what getting hitched involves.

MY FIRST POEM TO JUDITH

I thought I'd lost it. At one time it was in a collection of my early poems that I have despite being a little embarrassed by how bad some of them are, but when I looked, it wasn't there. Then I found it among some papers but lost it again. Then in a folder of old things, I found it. It was on typing paper. Remember typing paper, somewhat parchmenty so you could erase (and I needed to erase a lot.)

The paper was folded in threes the way you do to put something in a business envelope. So it may have been sent off somewhere and came back with a rejection slip. Remember those days you older ones? No Submittable, no email internet stuff, just the mailman making his rounds. He came around twice a day when I was young. Hope and expectation was alive then, not this deluge of any-time-of-day correspondence.

There it was, the first poem I wrote for Judith. We had met at the Breadloaf Writer's conference the previous summer, but now she was visiting me in New Jersey. We were staying with friends in Farmingdale, not that far from the shore and I took her to Asbury Park a boardwalky resort that I hung out in with my family when I was young.

On Valentine's Day, I've given a poetry reading for more than 30 years. Usually about 100 attend. This year I told Judith I had a special Valentine for her, but I wouldn't tell her what. I told what I've written above to the audience and read the following:

"Winter Visit [1961]"

That day the wind spun off the sea
And blew us close. We walked the rough
Geometry of boardwalk before
The boarded shells of summer pastimes.

The iced bones of the Ferris wheel
Circled above our heads; inside
The pavilion we kissed between the stalled
Merry-go-round and the lifeless pinball.

Then down and out to the water's edge
Where gulls watched silent from the pilings
As we left two still trails across
The sea's junkyard in their winter keeping.

Among the torn rags of weed and claw
You found a perfect curve of shell
Which somehow held us both alive
And soft in its smooth pearl hollow.

NOTES FROM MAYRHOFEN

[This was lost for years. I don't know why it did not make the transfer from one computer to the next. But a day or two ago, I found a hard copy and retyped while editing slightly. As I read, I am transported to that time and to the strange feeling of those days after the burning towers.]

I awoke yesterday morning wanting the breakfast at the Hotel Waldheim in Mayrhofen. It would have consisted of strong coffee, juice, cereal, a lovely roll, and great bread with slices of pungent cheese, salami, and something like a German Mortadella. I guess my hunger means it's time to get my notes in order. I like to do sort of word-sketches when I travel.

After the 9/11 attack, Judith and I found ourselves on the first Lufthansa flight out of San Francisco. We had planned with a dozen others to go hiking in the Austrian Alps for a holiday, but the exploding towers changed everything. All flights were cancelled, then they started again. Someone on television said that you should try your travel agent instead of the airline. So I called, found 2 tickets available on United instead of Lufthansa. I immediately took them and called our friends. They called, but there were no more seats. I had called at a lucky moment. And the Lufthansa flights and United flights were on the same plane.

We were told to arrive 4 hours early, the plane left 3 hours late. The place was packed with people hoping to get on standby, mostly Germans who had run out of money in San Francisco. The flight was packed and nervous. The security seemed appropriate. The flying time was long, tedious, and uncomfortable, the Germans allowing no extra room for the tall. A Flight Attendant let me sit in her bucket seat for

69

awhile until another one told me I was in the way of the emergency door. We flew to Munich and then trained to Mayrhofen, a ski town near Innsbruck. Judith and I were the only ones to arrive from America though one woman of our group had been already traveling in Europe. Our plans had been made with an English hiking company and the English had no serious trouble with their travel. Judith had people to hike with. I was no longer able to hike. So while Judith walked the Alps, I roamed the town.

9/17/01   Here's an amazing sight from my first day. While having lunch, I heard the sound of bells and I looked out of the door of the cafe and saw a dozen beautiful cows walking down the street covered with flowers, horns festooned with streamers of braided blossoms. The waitress said it was a ritual done each year as they brought down the cows from the high pastures to winter in the valley.

"Ritual"

Mid September early snow,—so,
from the high pastures a dozen cows,
horns streaming with flowers,
flowed with heavy grace down
a street lined with racks of discounted
summer clothes. Suddenly, all the shops
are ski shops.
                        Slowly the Green Year
walks down the mountain followed by her
attendants. She will leave them here
and follow the valley south. Praise her,
Bossy, Praise her Floribell, Praise her
you sweet ladies. May your winter barns
be full, the hands of your farmer warm.

"9/18 Traversing"

Early morning dark. I lie in bed
shades pulled back. Through the fog,
I see a sinuous twist of lights
tracing a road down the mountain.
Nothing straight here. What moves
must traverse the line of mountain
rock. Between up and down
one moves sidewise.

I had two special books with me, William Stafford's *The Way It Is* and Robert Bly's *Iron John* reissued after 10 years. (If you haven't read it since then, read it again. It's even better.)

"William Stafford in Mayrhofen"

He would have liked the muteness
of the morning fog, the light, the coffee.
He would have liked one piece of strudel
without the whipped cream. He would not
have bought a feathered hat, but would
have admired those who wore them.
Walking through the streets, he would
have understood the people.
Some he would have liked.

"Ongoingness"

Beneath the high thrust of snow, rock, ice—
small valley things—a wren in a tree full of pears,
a bee, warm in the afternoon sun tending
window box flowers, grass carrying on being grass.

Even the green
of the grass carries
autumnal darkness.

Night-snow crept down the mountain.
This morning, firs hurl back their green defense.
I think of how many strides my seven-league boots
would take to reach the sea.

I bought a lift ticket so I could get to the tops of the
mountains and so most days I would go up and have lunch
at one of the gasthauses, most often a cappuccino and a
strudel. Each place made its own strudel. Delicious. I read
a recipe of how to do it yesterday. Such a fuss for the crust,
such a delightful crust.

Light snack—
but the strudel has cream
and the coffee's topped mitt schlag.

"Gasthaus at the Top of the Lift"

Watching snow melt on a copper roof.
The slant is pleasing, almost Japanese.
Even the chimneys are copper and the water
sluices down into copper gutters and out
a copper pipe jutting out at the same
pleasing angle. Wind catches the water
blowing it into spray. The sun shines on all,
gleaming from the copper roof, gleaming
from the high mountain snow, shining
through the slow-gathering clouds.

The mountain brothers stand
white-shouldered before

the gathering clouds thinking
long, slow thoughts.

No valley perspective here.
The mountains stand in deep relief
like views from a stereopticon.
On each mountain, where the firs
give up trying, majesty asserts itself.

> The sky
> in the East, so blue
> in the West, so fierce.

"At the Hotel"

The proprietor's daughter behind the bar
tells of those coming down the high ski run
who fall, laughing, arms and skis in the air,
nylon rumps on the ice—then the slide,
and then—the slide.

"9/20   Below the Pinkerbahn"

I'm riding in the high air going higher.
Below, three farmers working a farm
that would slide down the hill if it could.
One drives his tractor in ever decreasing rectangles,
his machine leans away from the mountain,
> his body towards it.
The other two rake new-mown hay downward,
> each pull starting a green avalanche
> which comes to rest at a flattish place.
Surely here a farmer must have one long leg.

"On Top"

Each cow is belled with its own note.
Their coats, the shiny, slate-gray brown of
    Weimaraner.
They graze the high grass by the fence along the
    path.
A woman holds her child up to pet one cow's sweet
    head.
An immense tongue comes out to lick a red cheek.
I'm peaceful, but I've nothing like the cow's deep
    peace.

"On the Terrace"

At a gasthaus—high enough to bring me
eye to eye with the mountains,
a butterfly, a bee, and, in the shadows,
a wraith of melting snow.
Now two slender German women,
maybe in their 30s drinking tall beers.
Among all this gray, green, white,
and eternal blue, their lips burn red.

"9/21   First Day of Autumn"

I am full of fears.
Up the Ahornbahn
and at the top—I think
to go right back down.
Another part says "No!"
so I sit with strudel
and hot chocolate
breathing deeply.

"Later"

The first day of Fall.
The day seems calm,
yet the small leaves
of the pear tree
shimmer like
the wings of a butterfly.

AN ASSEMBLAGE OF CATHEDRALS

I find in an old notebook of dreams proof of the existence of God. The dream offers first a proposition, "Only God can create new matter. The rest of us must do with what's here." I want to add *already* but refuse to alter what dream has offered. Then my notebook goes on to say "Some sense in the dream that new matter is entering the universe—Therefore...."

Well there you are. If one, then the other, and "Therefore" again. Simple. Well....

A while ago, a bit of Debussy was playing so I think now of his "Sunken Cathedral." Much nicer in French, *La Cathédrale Engloutie.* When you think of it, it seems to rise from the depths and brings friends along. Here are some:

Fire at Notre Dame, What I find myself grieving for the most are the thousand-year-old oak beams that held up the spire. Did I read somewhere that that area was called the forest? And I grieve for the forests that will be needed for the restoration.

And yet, cathedrals are where you find them.

Beautiful my tanned hand upon the page—gray pen angled over thumb, under index, over middle finger. Eye admires what it sees and sees more than we admire. So, I look at my white comforter rising like Mont Blanc above my knees and the heap of yesterday's shirt and pants convoluted as a Kraken at the foot of my bed.

The bed sits four-cornered as the earth before Columbus set off on his roundabout way. Now my simple shuttered windows rise like the stained glass of cathedrals and my heart unclenches, loving even the pane with the elegant web where the spider sucks on her morning fly.

"Easter Saturday"

Walking the dog
in a cathedral of an afternoon,
not gothic, roman—sky a blue dome
held up by north south east and west.

Even the distant freeway traffic
sounds hushed like the way we talk
in a place that feels sacred.

The dog, however, is as interested
in earthly things as ever. He gives
a worldly woof then me a look that says
"What is, is. No need to get poetical."
He's got a good case, and, yet,
it is a cathedral of an afternoon.

A MEMORABLE FANCY

A friend reads a poem that ends "but the word had
courage." I thought about that and thought about words
and thought that a word is hurt when it is used hatefully.

Sometimes, maybe not enough, I listen to my thoughts and
wonder what they mean. I think now that words are spirit,
children of the human spirit, the first ones were born with
the naming of things.

Words have a lifetime and many are gone forever along
with the language that mothered them.

Words get old, twenty three skidoo to you. Some go on
forever, I, am.

I think of *freedom*. I used to love that word. Still do. But
every time I hear it used to conceal some slavery, I feel for it,
feel I must apologize to it, explain that it is not at fault, we are.

Then mind flew to this old poem of mine which is only
obliquely connected, but it came unbidden and I must let it
say hello.

> "Dirty"
>
> The dirty joke sighs.
> It knew midway
> it was in the wrong place.
>
> "I'm just a string of words,"
> the joke says defensively,
> "It's not my fault
> he's got a tin ear."

But the dirty joke knows
it can't be unsaid,
so it hangs in the air
defiantly like soot.

THOUGHTS OF A NON-NONE

There's that list of religions from which we're offered a choice. If none of them quite fit, at the bottom there's *None*. Well that's not for me either so I've taken to calling myself a Non-None. My religious feeling is not defined by any of the above, but it certainly is not defined by *None*. Thoughts:

While knotting my shoes, which gets harder as I get older, I realized that if I were Catholic I would prefer to go to a church, well, cathedral really, in which the mass was sung in Latin. I've sung many of the great mass settings in Latin, and I know enough Latin to understand what I'm singing and conductors always insist on singers having a sense of what the sounds coming out of their mouths mean, but while tying my shoes I realized that I didn't care about understanding. What I wanted was the incantatory sound, the glorious AH of *Ave,* the dark EH of *Requiem,* the round OH of *Gloria.* It was the sound that penetrated me, the sound of what has sometimes been called "the holy vowels"—think of the OM sound that some feel is the heartbeat of the universe. How rich it is to say, richer even in a chant. Some would say, and I for the moment agree, it is an all-encompassing sound. So maybe an understanding the words of the mass gets in the way of the mass. I don't insist on this, but wonder.

"Remember the ending of Hopkins' "God's Grandeur?""

And for all this, nature is never spent;
There lives the dearest freshness deep down things;
And though the last lights off the black West went
Oh, morning, at the brown brink eastward, springs —
Because the Holy Ghost over the bent

World broods with warm breast and with ah!
    bright wings.

How great that *ah!* is. It is an *Ah* of Awe, and we feel the awe deep down, and the exhalation of our saying is prayer. (I admit that it's good to understand the words of Hopkins that bring us to that great sound then releases us from it.)

I think we have lost the feeling of awe and so the universe we live in has grown smaller except for the astrophysicists who seem to understand the universe as a vast cathedral. Once here on earth we found the language of awe. That language was the cathedral. It spoke our feeling of awe and also recreated it in us. (Yes, there are smaller spaces that offer their version of that experience and if we use eyes and ears, nature too enjoys building cathedrals. Maybe there's nothing that's not.)

"Today I Vote for Awe"

One day an ancestor picked up a stone,
found it comforting, useful. What to do,
but start noticing the world as something
other than food and fear. World asked us, then,
to keep track—"Draw on walls of caves," it said,
offering us charcoal and ocherous pigments.
As bison and reindeer leapt out of our hands
they called out "Look inside too."
Awe became God, then, with her many stories
to tell the children—or was She/He there all along
waiting for someone to talk with.

"How To Build a Cathedral"

The leaves outside my window shake with a deeper
movement than the continuing ripple of the morning,
midsummer breeze. "Squirrels," I think, and think
of how I know they're there although I cannot see them,
not a large movement, but enough if you pay
attention. This is how the ancients found the holy places,
then followed the ley lines that led from one to another.
"Ah," you say, then "Ah" again, if you are paying
attention and mark where you are. Maybe you leave
a stone you've carried because it felt good in your hand.
Another person does the same. Soon there's a cairn,
then a cathedral where boys like me pay no
attention, but sing the mass beautifully anyway.

"A Riff on Alleluia"

Four open vowels beginning with the openest, *ah,*
        the one the doctor tells you to say so he can
            look
        all the way down your throat,
then next *leh* as in *lent,* a little bit more forward
        in the mouth,
then even more forward, *lu,* mouth pursed
        as if to whistle,
then a retreat for the *yah* like the turn that makes
        a dance a dance.

Tongue has been dancing, the elegant dance of *ahs* and *ells,*
three steps forward and a *yah* turning back, showing off,
enjoying the supple life. Cheeks are the *corps de ballet,* back,
outward, forward and back.

Say it a few times and pay attention to what's going on in

your mouth, the pleasures of the movement of your mouth.

Alleluia the easiest and loveliest word to sing.
It invites your tongue to dance and you to music.
Hallelujah is Forceful, Political, Marching Orders,
but *Alleluia* is lyrical, introverted, joyful.

"Theogony"

Adam created god in what he thought was his own
image.

Eve, mischievous, created Olympus and all its noisy
bickerers. Then she whispered you can find smaller
powers too if you look where roads cross or listen
to the secret hum of trees.

Earth brought forth Pan, hairy-legged, horned, but
humanish. He played music and danced on his goat
feet out of his exuberance at being alive.

"Again Walking My Dog"

Great gray early spring morning,
low-hanging clouds beneath a wash of blue.
Somewhere behind them the sun must shine
    for the creation shimmers in the mildest of golds.
I walk in a wonder, not skeptic, not agnostic, nor
    exactly believer—

My dog pulls this way and that against her leash.
This is her time, really. She shares it with me.
She is interested in all things with a tail to nose passion.
I follow with my arm and eye where she leads,

to the holes of ground squirrels,
    the leavings of previous dogs tufts of
        delicious young grass.
Now I'm pulled sideways by her lunge
    towards the black, awkward ducklike birds
        that quickly waddle into the pond.
Being farther from the ground, I see more, and less.

I am a middle creature, then, half way between.

The clouds move fast overhead in a high wind, though
down here the air is still,—damp as if rain will come.
A whoosh of cars rebounds from the freeway
    soundwall.
If I closed my eyes, I can imagine the sea.

"What should such creatures as I do, crawling
between earth and heaven?" Hamlet cried.
I wonder the same in a quieter non-despairing way.

My dog barks her confident bark.
She says the world is and is and is—
but I am a middle creature, halfway between—

Contorno

The side dish,
which can be a salad
or cooked vegetables

ON KEEPING YOUR OLD NOTEBOOKS

Mary Oliver on keeping a journal: "For at least 30 years,
and at almost all times, I have carried a notebook with me,
in my back pocket. It has always been the same kind of
notebook—small, 3" x 5", and handsewn.

What I write down is extremely exacting terms of phrasing
and or cadence. In an old notebook I can find, 'look the
trees / are turning / their own bodies / into pillars of light.'"

I started keeping a notebook sixty years ago at the
suggestion of a therapist who wanted me to keep track
of my dreams. My first had ordinary paper, but I came
to like the feel of good paper and I switched to ones with
paper of almost watercolor quality. So they're filled with
doodles and sketches as well as the messings about with
poems—writing, rewriting, abandoning. I have maybe a
100 scattered about my retirement flat. Treasure chests. So
here's a few pages with a little touching up.

The feet of the young girl running over the grass
in the neighborhood park touch the earth lightly, lightly.
Her young mother, heavy with her next child, looks
at her smiling, and I smile as I walk past in the early
evening of a late August. The girl has hardly rump
enough to give her shorts purchase. Her mother's breasts,
full and round with the coming of milk, overflow
their halter. She sighs as the daughter skips to the fountain,
  sips, then scurries back
with one, two, three cartwheelshurling herself down in a
  heap of ankles, knees,
elbows by her mother's side. I am some place beneath
  thinking, a walker and a
watcher, drifting in the late summer nowhere to go and going

CODA

The notebook is a score of years old. Now, likely, the girl's
grown and gone, along with her not-yet born brother or
sister. The mother may be a grandmother.

My bad knee makes walking difficult. It is October in this
now, and yet, and yet, then is still then and they are still
there in my notebook as am I—walking by.

FROM ANOTHER

Books fail. So I look out of the window
at the gray morning sky though a tracery
of twig, leaf, and the last berries of autumn
and think of the conflict between word and eye.
Neither quite has room for the other, yet I know
I cannot see without words. Earlier I read
that the sense impressions of one-celled animals
are not edited for something like a brain, "that only
the simplest animals perceive the universe as it is."
I read somewhere else that the invention of glass,
something to see through, separated us from the world.
So, we live in a house that eye and word have together built
out of planks made of guesses about the immensity.

Twenty years later I find most of this in a notebook, read
it with pleasure finding myself comfortable in this house
looking out of the window into another gray sky. And
I see that once again I've used the word *tracery* which I
first heard in the spring of 1951 in a story written by Joan
Kennedy for a writing class. I remember loving the word
and now I remember her long, narrow intelligent attractive
face and going with her to the spring gardenia dance where
we talked much, danced little.

"SCORPIO (Oct. 23 – Nov 20): In their book, *An Incomplete Education,* Judy Jones and William Wilson list the favorite colors of famous poets. T. S. Eliot loved eggplant, sable, and mustard. Wallace Stevens preferred vermillion, chartreuse and wine, while Ezra Pound liked ivory and jade. In light of current astrological omens, which are nudging you in the direction of greater subtlety and precision, I urge you to draw inspiration from these poets' lyrical tastes. Refine your definitions of your favorite everything, Scorpio: colors, smells, feelings, tastes, physical sensations, tones of voice, types of wind, qualities of light—everything."

When I was a boy, my favorite colors came from the sound of their names on my packet of Crayolas—burnt umber, raw umber, burnt sienna, red ochre. The sounds fascinated and lured me to those colors. Maybe that was my first connection with word sounds as interesting outside of the realm of the nursery rhyme.

ANOTHER NOTE FROM THE SCORE OF YEARS OLD NOTEBOOK

Morning and the things of the world look at me
in their solid way—the clear-glassed coffee mug,
the round silver cylinder thermos, the brown desk
my parents gave me when I turned 12, the ball point
in my hand. The hand too is solid, but differently so,
and I think of the glass in the window flowing downward
as surely as water though it will take a thousand years
to get to the sea.

It is good to rise again with [sounds (poems?) in harmony
with?] to sing with the morning light. Shall we rise three

notes above tonic in a major mode or are we a two and a
half minors this morning? this foggy morning's full of sweet
sounds, the best of them not yet words   so we'll hum

Mary Oliver: "The words do not take me to the reason I
made the entry, but back to the felt experience, whatever it
was. This is important. I can, then, think forward again to
the idea—that is, the significance of the event rather than
back upon it. It is the instant I try to catch in the notebooks,
not the comment, not the thought."

I RODE HORSES, YOU READ BOOKS.

I used to tell my creative writing classes the artistic form that came the closest to depicting the lives we lead was the soap opera—because, as in the soap opera, we all have many stories going on at the same time. Some are short, some are like lyrics in tone and length, some go on and on, drop into the background, and are revived later when some necessity draws them forth—Uncle Ned goes off to explore the Amazon Jungle and comes back three years later just in time to make the wedding legal. This story of mine is long in years, short in hours.

Small Kentucky college. 25th Reunion. I gave a reading of poems and stories about love. Peterson Pontificates on Love trumpeted the college paper. Many old friends came and came up on to the stage afterwards. So, up comes this beautiful woman, catches my eye, says "Hi." I say, "Hi." She says, "Hi. Do you remember me?" and in the silence—"Do you remember me? I'm Patsy." Indeed it was. I said "Hi," kissed her on the cheek, turned to cut off my other conversations so we could really talk, turn back, and she's gone. "Patsy," I holler into the cavernous auditorium, "Patsy," but she really is gone. To myself I say, "Peterson, you've done it again."

I got her phone number from the alumni office and called and called, even at 5:30 in the morning, but she was never in. I finally did connect and she explained that she was off fox hunting the morning I called so early. We made a date for that night to meet for dinner and went to a restaurant where her son was a waiter (she had had two sons from a marriage that didn't last). He raised an eyebrow as he shook my hand. We went back to her place and talked for a long time. Here's from a poem I wrote about the experience,

What the young offer each other
is the marvelous future, all that can happen,
all that will be. Older, suspicious of promises,
we learn to offer what we have lived.
It is a smaller, harder gift, yet beautiful like fact.

We wrote back and forth and then lost touch again, but
10 years later I went back to my 35th reunion and we
reconnected, the talk as easy and as good as it had been the
decade before. It was convenient for me to spend the night
at her house, but I had to get up early. She was going fox
hunting again. So, October dark, five in the morning, she
in her hunting outfit and a dungareed helper got her horse
into its trailer and set off. I followed in my rental car.

There were forty or fifty people, maybe more, in black caps,
red coats, white trousers and black boots getting ready to
ride at this beautiful Kentucky farm. There was a blessing
from a robed local priest. Everyone had a stirrup cup of
sherry before setting off. Someone was missing, so I helped
serve, reaching a silver salver of small glasses up to the
riders on the horses. The riders were ready, the hounds
were ready, and the fox, well there wasn't really a fox.
Someone had prepared a trail of fox scent for the hounds to
follow. I was glad to hear that, remembering Oscar Wilde's
line about fox hunting in England, "the unspeakable in
pursuit of the uneatable." I stood and watched as they all
set off, hounds, horses, riders, and Patsy. And that was my
last sight of her.

But not quite. The story hasn't ended. Remember that son
who raised his eyebrow? Well, I received a note from him
on Message. I responded and he gave me Patsy's phone
number. I called and we talked, she a widow, I a widower.
And so we began talking again, old people talk. She told
me about her good second marriage. He had even built a

barn for her where she could keep horses. She was living now in their big house, no other houses in sight but with a couple acres of lawn that she enjoyed mowing. I pictured her perched like a horseback rider on the mower as it went round and round. I shared things about living in a senior residence and my long marriage, the ways in which it got better and better as the years went by.

She welcomed my calls. I was someone she could talk to about the thises and thats of her life. I felt the same. I don't retain jokes but I have a friend who always has a new one and I would get one from him before I called because she liked to laugh. I'd call once or twice a week. Then she came to visit her son who, as it turns out, lives in the same city as I do. This is what I wrote about the visit.

"On Friday I had a wonderful talk. It was with my first real girlfriend, Patsy. We got together in the fall of 1953 at my small Kentucky college. I mentioned our coming meeting to a friend here at my retirement home. She warned me "You're going to see an old woman though you remember a young one." I replied "Well, she's going to see an old man." Yes, there was an old woman and an old man there, but also a young man and a young woman and the four of us had a good time being and seeing both, remembering about the ways and wanderings of our lives. Patsy summed it up by saying 'I rode horses, you read books.'" Not exactly right, but also exactly right.

As we sat waiting for her son to come and carry her off again, Patsy suggested we sing "Somewhere Over the Rainbow." We had both been in the choir, and so we did. I suggested we sing "For All We Know, We May Never Meet Again." We did know, we did know how unlikely that would be. Flying had become hard for both of us. But then all of our meetings had been unlikely. "We come, we go, like the ripples on a stream...."

In the fall she mentioned that she was losing weight, and later that she felt tired. She had liked the life at my senior residence and liked my apartment and began to think of moving to such a place. I encouraged her. Then it was discovered that she had a serious cancer. She was moved to a nursing home. The last time we talked, her daughter-in-law had to hold the phone to her ear.

In our last real talk together, she shared a memory of that time at the fox hunt. It had just come back to her. She remembered that before she rode off, I stood by her horse, reached up my hand, and rested it on the neck of her horse. I have always been somewhat afraid around big animals, yet I swear so fiercely did her remembrance come back to me that I could feel the neck of the horse beneath my hand as I looked up at Patsy all costumed and ready to ride.

A MEMORABLE FANCY

Thinking of the Models of Matisse

What to make of all these naked ladies some
in blue, some lined out—legs crossed, one arm
behind the head to shift the weight of one breast up-
ward, while the other hangs out with gravity.

Their faces are abstracted, introspective—
"Well, this is what the old guy wants,"
they seem to say. "Well, I'll give it to him.
He's paying—If he wants shape, I'll give

him shape, the old cut-up, but nothing
else of me." The Master nods his head,
points his beard harrumphs "Don't move,"
and though the rump on which most of

their weight rests aches, they're still till the scissors
are done, or his blue brush, or his sure, inky line.

There was a moment when Matisse's models went on strike
and put their clothes back on. Matisse said, "Ladies, what
are you doing? Please take off your clothes off so I can get
back to work," but they refused. "This is ridiculous," he
said, "I pay by the hour, but I only pay when you're naked."
Still they refused. "How can we work this out?"

Odette spoke for them all, "We will all take off our clothes
and let you draw us after you take off your clothes and
let us draw you." Matisse, brooding, said, "All right, but
I've got to put my hat on." They agreed—he took off his
clothes—put on his hat—and sat on a stool. The women
scurried around, found things to draw with and paper draw

on. When they finished, Matisse got dressed and the models got undressed.

Odette insisted that she had drawn the best hat.

KNIGHT OF THE CART

...another kind of net, that language, the one the world
gives us to cast so that we might catch in it a little of what
it is and what we are, and we are, among other things,
the poverties of the language we inherit. Robert Hass,
"Families and Prisons," *What Light Can Do.*

These days when night and cold come so soon one wants
nothing more than to huddle around a fire, read for a
while, then go to bed, though the world surrounds us with
obligations. I was walking the dog in the cold night air,
almost remembering what I wanted to remember, and then
it came, the opening paragraph of James Joyce's "Araby."

The first time I read it was magic. The feel and look of
autumn air were there and the intensity of the awareness of
one's aliveness.

> When the short days of winter came, dusk fell
> before we had well eaten our dinners. When we
> met in the street the houses had grown sombre.
> The space of sky above us was the colour of ever-
> changing violet and towards it the lamps of the
> street lifted their feeble lanterns. The cold air stung
> us and we played till our bodies glowed. Our
> shouts echoed in the silent street. The career of
> our play brought us through the dark muddy lanes
> behind the houses, where we ran the gauntlet of
> the rough tribes from the cottages, to the back
> doors of the dark dripping gardens where odours
> arose from the ashpits, to the dark odorous stables
> where a coachman smoothed and combed the horse
> or shook music from the buckled harness. When
> we returned to the street, light from the kitchen

windows had filled the areas. If my uncle was seen
turning the corner, we hid in the shadow until we
had seen him safely housed. Or if Mangan's sister
came out on the doorstep to call her brother in to
his tea, we watched her from our shadow peer up
and down the street. We waited to see whether
she would remain or go in and, if she remained,
we left our shadow and walked up to Mangan's
steps resignedly. She was waiting for us, her figure
defined by the light from the half-opened door. Her
brother always teased her before he obeyed, and
I stood by the railings looking at her. Her dress
swung as she moved her body, and the soft rope of
her hair tossed from side to side.

Yes, the paragraph described me too, though I was far in
time and space from "dark odorous stables." (Actually,
there were some old stables around where I lived, used for
garages for awhile, but now mostly storage sheds filled with
mysterious things.)

Then I remembered the girl next door, a year or two older
than me who had once been the baby sitter for me and
my brother, but when I had caught up a little bit, passed
puberty, and we were both going to high school, she walked
ahead of me all the way while I shuffled behind and never
said a word. But I certainly thought of her in my own way.

Joyce goes on to say:

Her image accompanied me even in places the most
hostile to romance. On Saturday evenings when my
aunt went marketing I had to go to carry some of
the parcels. We walked through the flaring streets,
jostled by drunken men and bargaining women,
amid the curses of labourers, the shrill litanies of

shop-boys who stood on guard by the barrels of pigs' cheeks, the nasal chanting of street- singers, who sang a come-all-you about O'Donovan Rossa, or a ballad about the troubles in our native land. These noises converged in a single sensation of life for me: I imagined that I bore my chalice safely through a throng of foes I did not know whether I would ever speak to her or not or, if I spoke to her, how I could tell her of my confused adoration. But my body was like a harp and her words and gestures were like fingers running upon the wires.

Years ago, remembering watching a girl in my 6th grade class doing fractions at the blackboard (her blouse always separated from her skirt revealing a little bit of flesh), I wrote:

I have never seen flesh
that I wanted more than that thin
triangle of light brown back. What
did I want? I did not know but
at night when I lay in bed the thought of her
doing simple fractions would crack me open
and I knew there was something I had to have
that not to have it would be like death
or worse than death because I would be
alive and know I didn't have it—something
so huge, so tremendous, so
wonderful my body could not
contain it and it surrounded me like
phosphorescence. This is my soul
something wanted to say but that was far
from what I had been taught and the word
was confusing—and what to do with these feelings
more so.

As we grow older, I think we forget the connection between soul and flesh, between body and spirit, and how the grown-world's definitions can drive us to speechlessness. Well, when we can't talk using the language of words, we speak with the action of gesture.

You'll remember Mangan's sister almost casually asks the narrator if he's going to Araby, a bazaar downtown, and he can do nothing but answer yes, and so he must go, though all the easily-made promises of the world conspire against his going being easy. But now it is a knight's quest.

I recently found the following in a book I kept when trying to write a poem each day. This morning, I rewrote the last four lines:

Mangan's sister, the light from her house
shining through her hair. "Are you going
to Araby?" she asks—so "Yes," we must say
and board the tram to Vanity Fair watching
the large Peterson and the small Peterson
looking at each other appalled, each asking
the other "How can you be so foolish?"

Yet now I say thanks be for holy desire,
and thanks to that young self for carrying
it through the marketplace because
he had said yes to one of Mangan's sisters.

Though at the end the boy feels himself "a creature driven and derided by vanity," and his eyes burn "with anguish and anger," it was the right thing to have done and when I finally allowed myself to be that foolish, it was the right thing for me too.

As to the title of this piece. It is from the Arthurian legends.

Guenevere has been captured. Launcelot has gone off to rescue her. His horse is killed. A dwarf comes by driving a cart used to carry prisoners. Though he needs a ride, he hesitates for a fraction of a second before he gets on the cart because his knighthood will be tarnished from such a ride. Guenevere sees this, and for that slight hesitation puts Launcelot through all kinds of hell even as he goes about the business of rescuing her. That slight hesitation was an offense against courtly love, the putting of one's reputation, what the world thinks of one, above one's duty to the beloved. How human I find all this.

Dolce

AND FROM JUDITH, A VALENTINE

Morning, home after a long trip, you tell me—
"Nothing's more wonderful than waking up
by your side." A modest man, I look down
into my coffee cup—think of all the splendors
of the world, but, suddenly proud, I smile and think
well maybe, just maybe, mind,—it might be true,

and, now, remembering waking up by your side,
I'll say nothing was more wonderful than that.

A NOTE ON THE TYPE

My Dinner with Nils
is set in Sabon,
designed by Jan Tschichold in 1964.
The Roman design is inspired
by the typefaces
of Claude Garamond (c. 1480–1561),
especially a specimen
printed by Konrad Berner,
a printer from Frankfurt.
Berner had married the widow
of printer Jacques Sabon,
after whom the typeface is named.
This elegant, highly readable typeface
is ideal for poetry.

,